D0859678

Dropping In On... IRAN

Philip Bader

A Geography Series

THE ROURKE BOOK COMPANY, INC.
VERO BEACH, FLORIDA 32964

Printed in the United States of America

Library of Congress Cataloging-in-Publication Data

Bader, Philip, 1969-
Iran / Philip Bader.
p. cm. — (Dropping in on)
Includes index.
Audience: 4.
ISBN 1-55916-285-6
1. Iran—Juvenile literature. [1. Iran—Description and travel.] I. Title. II. Series.

DS254.75 .B33 2000
955—dc21

00–038722

Printed in the USA

Iran

Official Name: Islamic Republic of Iran

Area: 636,293 miles (1,622,099 square kilometers)

Population: 67,540,000

Capital: Tehran

Largest City: Tehran (pop. 12,000,000)

Highest Elevation: Mount Damavand, 18,603 feet (5,670 kilometers)

Official Language: Farsi

Major Religion: Shiite Muslim (95%)

Money: Rial

Form of Government: Islamic Republic

Flag:

TABLE OF CONTENTS

Our Blue Ball — The Earth

The Earth can be divided into two hemispheres. The word hemisphere means "half a ball"—in this case, the ball is the Earth.

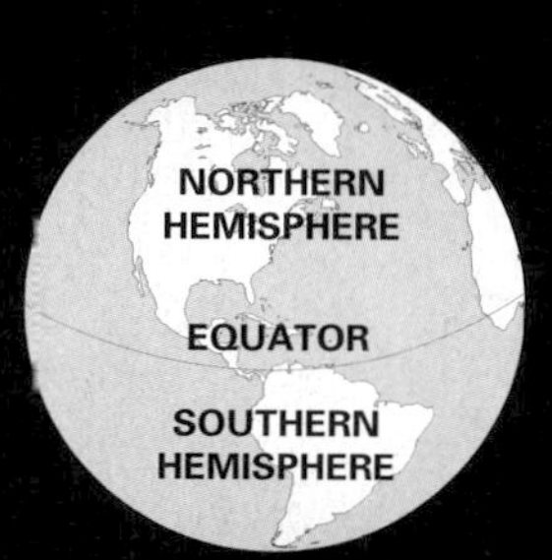

The equator is an imaginary line that runs around the middle of the Earth. It separates the Northern Hemisphere from the Southern Hemisphere. North America—where Canada, the United States, and Mexico are located—is in the Northern Hemisphere.

The Northern Hemisphere

When the North Pole is tilted toward the sun, the sun's most powerful rays strike the northern half of the Earth and less sunshine hits the Southern Hemisphere. That is when people in the Northern Hemisphere enjoy summer. When the

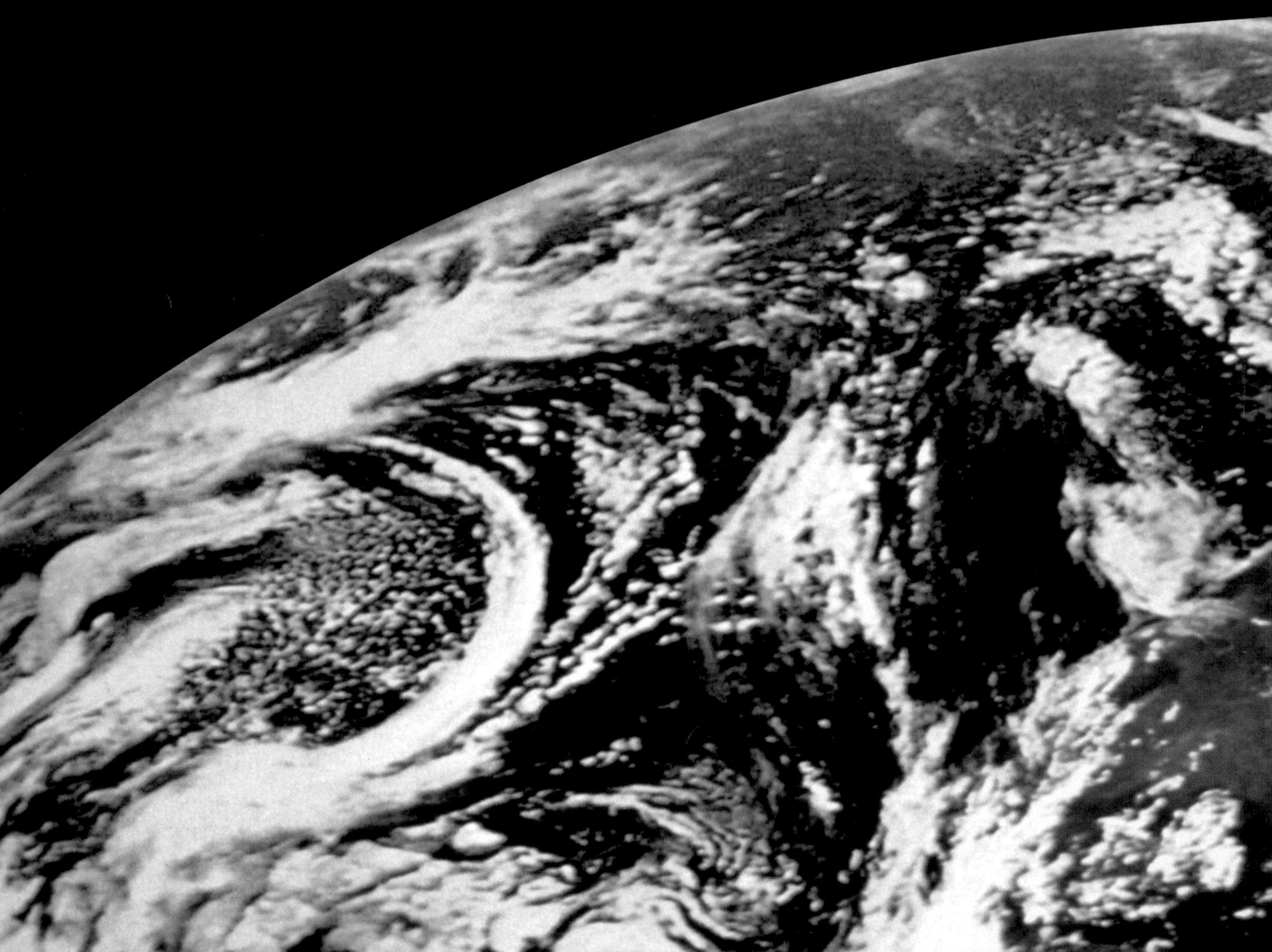

North Pole is tilted away from the sun and the Southern Hemisphere receives the most sunshine, the seasons reverse. Then winter comes to the Northern Hemisphere. Seasons in the Northern Hemisphere and the Southern Hemisphere are always opposite.

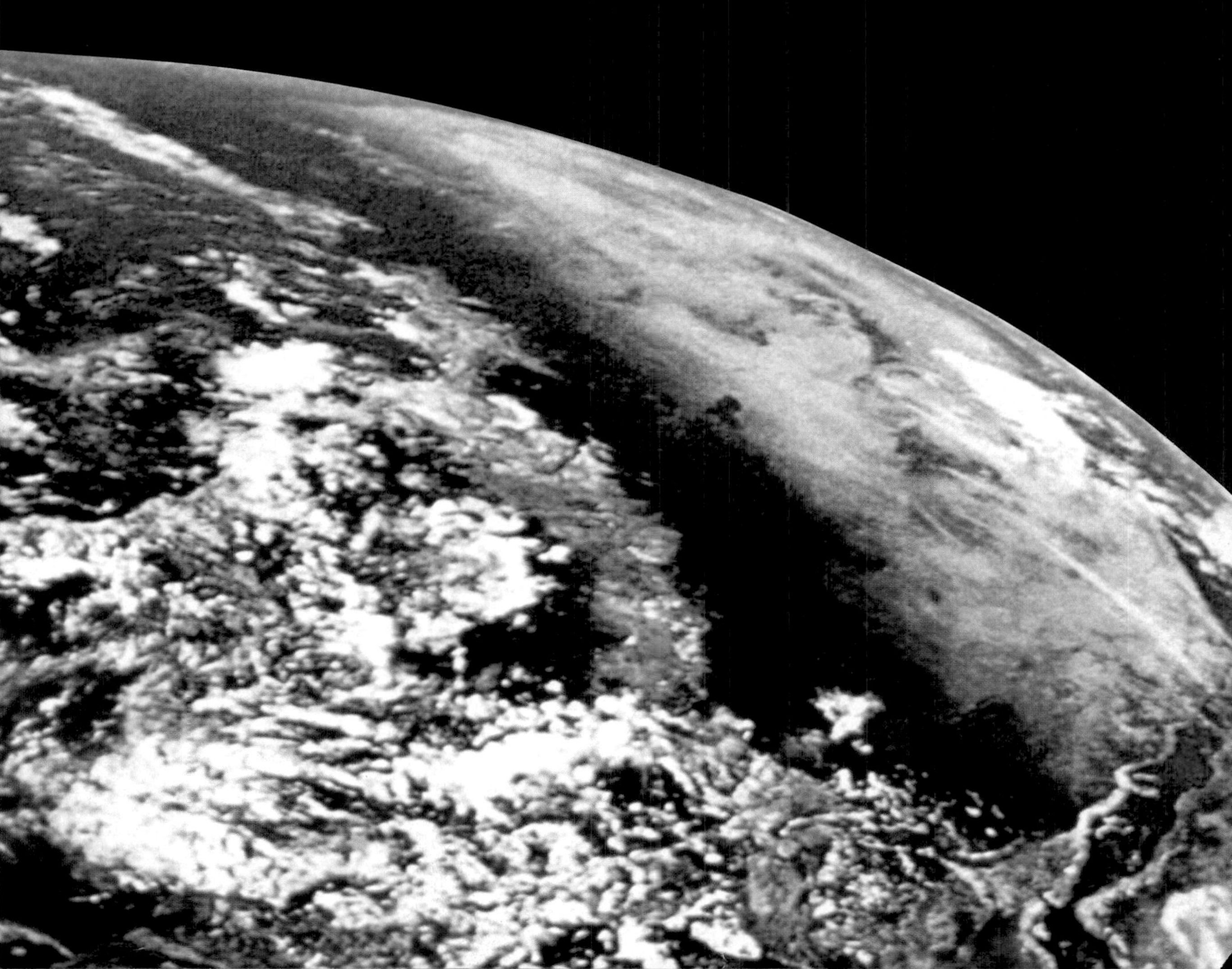

Get Ready for Iran

Let's take a trip! Climb into your hot-air balloon, and we'll drop in on a country located in an area of central Asia called the Middle East. Iran is bordered on the north by Armenia, Azerbaijan, Turkmenistan, and the Caspian Sea; on the west by Turkey and Iraq; on the east by Afghanistan and Pakistan; and to the south by the Persian Gulf. Iran was once called Persia, from the Persian Empire, which lasted from about 550 B.C.E. to 640 C.E.—nearly 1,200 years.

Seventy-five percent of Iran is covered by mountains and desert. Few people live in these regions, but they contain valuable natural resources. The Zagros Mountains in southwestern Iran are an important source for oil. Iran is the third largest producer of oil in the world.

Iran's mostly Muslim culture can appear strict and intolerant of western nations. Like other countries, Iran has had conflicts with its own people and those of neighboring countries. Current changes in the government, however, show that Iran's people are becoming more tolerant of other cultures and religions. Visitors to Iran will find most Iranians to be very generous hosts.

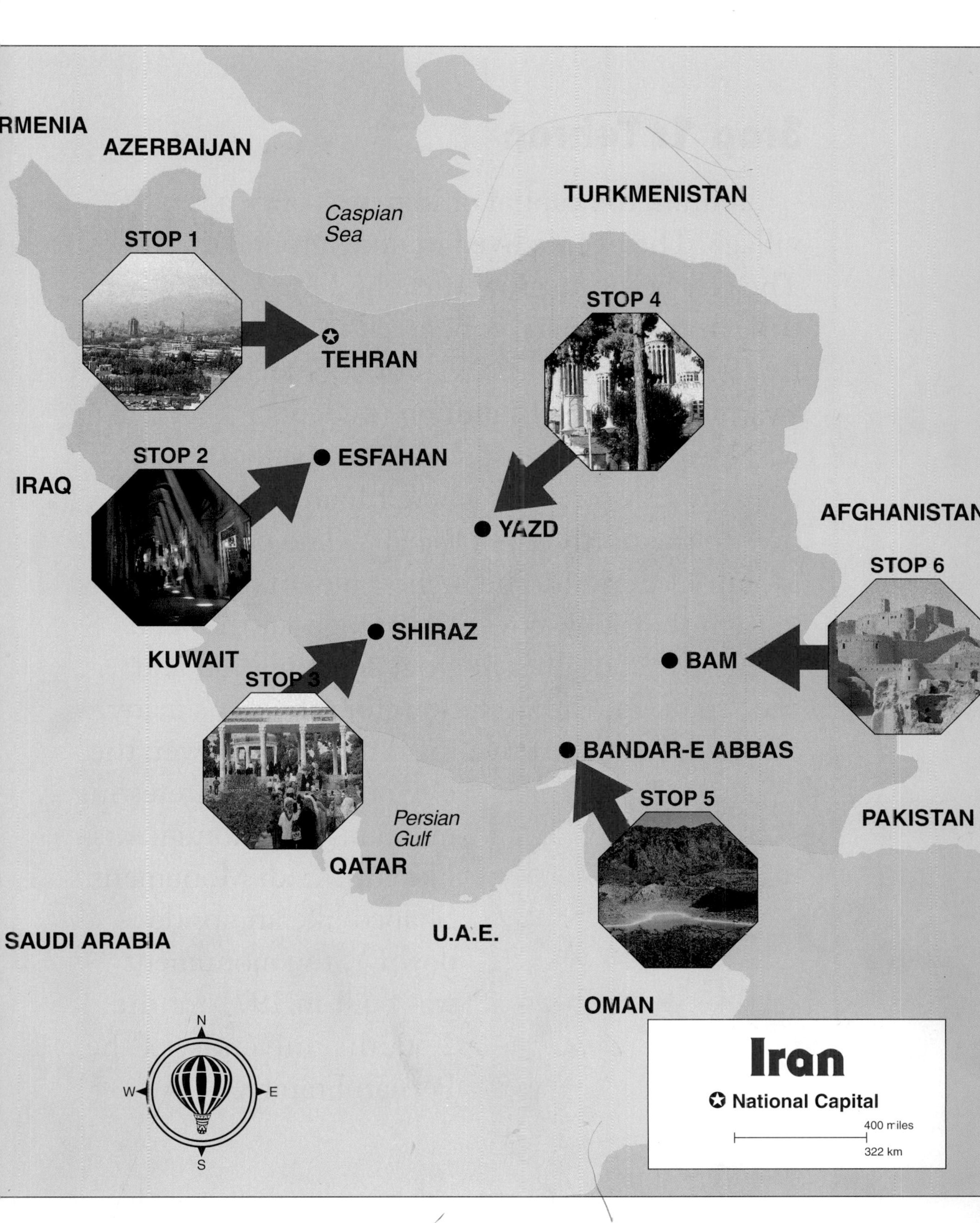
RMENIA
AZERBAIJAN
Caspian Sea
TURKMENISTAN
STOP 1
TEHRAN
STOP 4
STOP 2
ESFAHAN
IRAQ
YAZD
AFGHANISTAN
STOP 6
SHIRAZ
KUWAIT
BAM
STOP 3
BANDAR-E ABBAS
STOP 5
Persian Gulf
PAKISTAN
QATAR
SAUDI ARABIA
U.A.E.
OMAN
N
W
E
S
Iran
National Capital
400 miles
322 km

Stop 1: Tehran

Tehran, the capital of Iran, was once a small village. The people lived in underground dwellings. The city began to grow after the Mongols, a warrior tribe from East Asia, conquered the nearby city of Rey 900 years ago. Today Tehran, which means "warm slope," has 12 million residents.

Northern Tehran spreads into the foothills of the Alborz Mountains where Mount Damavand rises to the northeast of the city. The peak of Mount Damavand, the highest mountain in Iran, is so high that snow covers it throughout the year.

Tehran continues to grow in population and size. Traffic and air pollution from the city's many automobiles make traveling difficult. However, the city offers many interesting museums and monuments, like the Azadi Monument. Shaped like an upside-down Y, the monument was built in 1971 for the 2,500th anniversary of the Persian Empire.

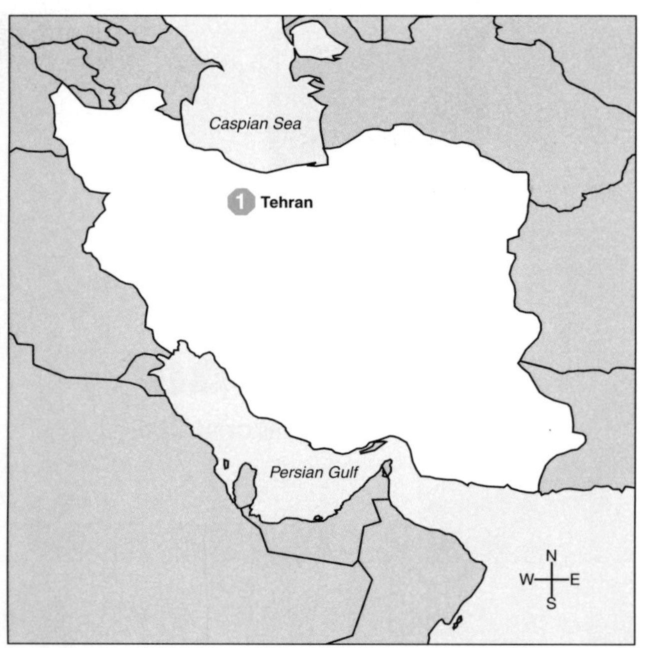

*Now let's fly **south-east** to Esfahan.*

An overview of the sprawling capital city of Tehran. In the summer, smog can be a problem for Tehran's 12 million residents.

Stop 2: Esfahan

In the Dasht-e-Kavir desert in central Iran, bright blue tiles cover the rooftops of Esfahan's religious buildings. The city used to be the capital of the Safavid Empire, which ruled Iran 500 years ago. Then, palaces bordered wide, tree-lined avenues, and elaborate bridges were built across the Zayande River, which runs through the city.

Today, many of these sites remain. The most important of these is the Great Mosque, completed in 1638. Covered inside and out with bright blue tiles, it seems to change color as sunlight strikes the building from different angles.

Esfahan also has one of the oldest and largest *bazaars* in Iran, called the Royal Bazaar. A bazaar is like a shopping mall but much larger. The Royal Bazaar runs for several miles through Esfahan. Tea shops, bathhouses, and gardens can be found among the twisting corridors of the bazaar.

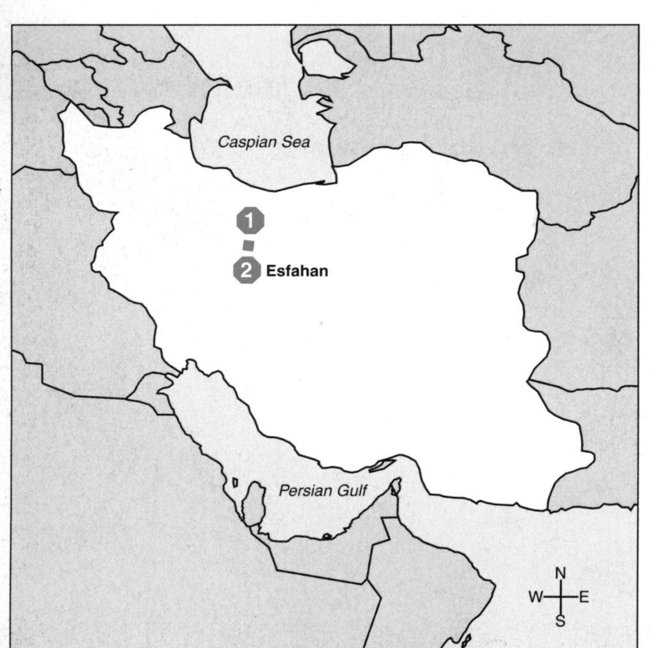

Now let's fly ***south*** *to Shiraz.*

Sunbeams shine through portholes in the ceiling of Esfahan's bazaar. Right: The south gate of the Great Mosque in Esfahan.

Persian Carpet Making

For 2,000 years, weavers in Iran have produced handmade carpets. Centuries ago, these carpets were so valuable that they were sometimes used as money. Kings throughout Europe and as far away as China desired them for their royal palaces.

Persian carpets are usually made from dyed wool that is hand-woven on a loom. Some carpet makers use silk. Silk carpets are often used as decorations or as ceremonial rugs during prayer. Early carpet designers used geometric and floral patterns to symbolize the beauty of Persian gardens. Later designs used verses from the Qur'an (pronounced kuh-RAN), the holy book of Islam.

As the demand increases for Persian carpets, fewer of them are made by hand. Machines have replaced looms, allowing carpetmakers to produce more carpets in a shorter amount of time. The ancient methods of weaving by hand are now taught to fewer people, and soon they may be lost completely.

Above: Shoppers examine the many styles of Persian carpets at an international carpet exhibition in Iran.

Right: A man dyeing wool in the bazaar at Esfahan. Dyed wool has been used in Persian carpet making for centuries.

Visitors walk through the gardens and tomb of the poet Hafiz in Shiraz.

Stop 3: Shiraz

Shiraz sits in a valley near the Zagros Mountains in southern Iran. Persians first settled this region. Later it became the center of two powerful empires, the Achaemenian and Sassanian. In the 7th century, Shiraz was known for its artists and scholars. They built beautiful *mosques* and gardens and wrote some of Iran's greatest poetry.

The poet Hafiz, whose name means "One who can recite the Qur'an from memory," lived and wrote in Shiraz 650 years ago. His poetry became famous throughout the country and then the world. The tomb and gardens built in his honor are among the city's most visited sites.

Shiraz continues to attract students and scholars, who come to the city to learn English at the university. The city also attracts many tourists. On the outskirts of Shiraz, an ancient Persian king named Darius began to build a mighty fortress.

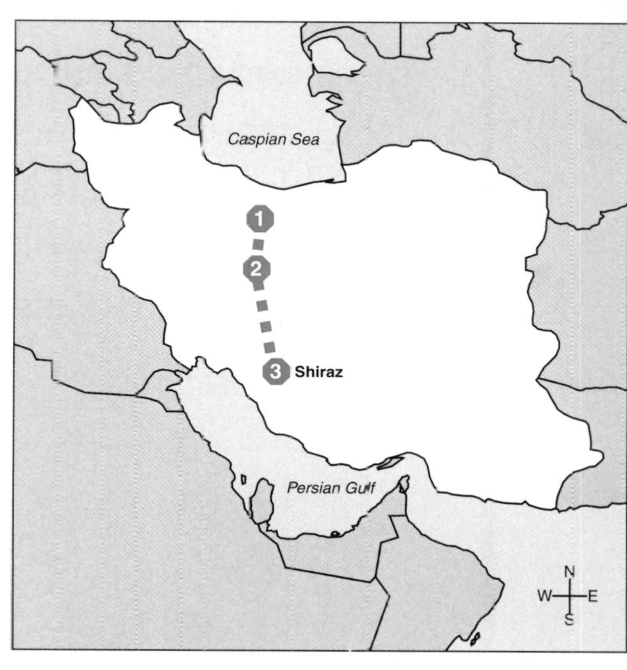

Now let's fly ***north-east*** *to Yazd.*

Persepolis

In the foothills of the Zagros Mountains east of Shiraz, King Darius I, the ruler of the Achaemenian Empire, began building Persepolis in 512 B.C.E. Over the next 150 years, later kings continued the work until its completion. The original city covered 125,000 square meters.

Artists carved images into stone stairways throughout the city. These figures, called *reliefs*, showed the many nationalities that made up the Achaemenian Empire. The largest building in Persepolis was the Hall of 100 Columns, where Darius I held receptions and met with his military advisers.

In 331 B.C.E., Alexander the Great conquered Persepolis, and it burned to the ground. The city's ruins remained buried under earth and sand until 1930, when archaeologists rediscovered them. Both the National Museum of Iran in Tehran and the smaller Persepolis Museum display many valuable artifacts discovered in the ruins of the ancient city.

Xerxes' Porch in the ancient city of Persepolis. (Inset): A view of Darius's Palace in ancient Persepolis.

Stop 4: Yazd

Yazd, the oldest inhabited city in Iran, is surrounded by deserts: the Dasht-e-Kavir to the north, and the Dasht-e-Lut to the south. In order to survive the extreme heat in the summer, ancient builders designed wind towers called *badgirs*. These towers caught the slightest breeze and funneled it to the living areas of the house.

Before the Arab conquest brought Islam to Iran, Zoroastrianism was the main religion. A number of ancient Zoroastrian buildings still stand in Yazd, including the Towers of Silence. There, dead bodies were exposed to *scavengers*.

Two thousand years ago, builders in Yazd designed a system of underground tunnels, called *ghanats*, to make use of underground water sources. Though modern methods of water supply have replaced many of the tunnels, ghanats are still used throughout Iran.

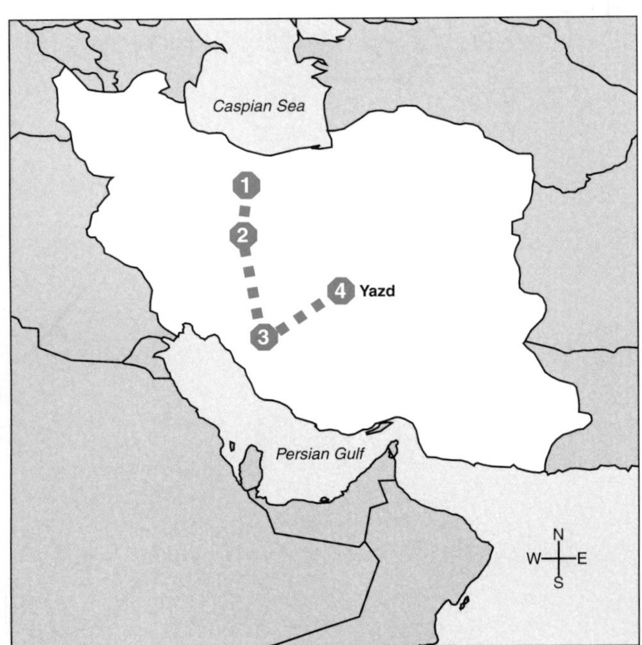

Now let's fly ***south*** *to Bandar-e Abbas.*

The ancient builders of Yazd used wind towers to bring cool breezes into the living areas of houses. These towers, like those pictured here, are still in use today.

Growing Up in Iran

Islam is an important part of everyday life for families in Iran. From an early age, children learn to read and understand the Qur'an, the holy book of Islam. School attendance is not mandatory in Iran, but 95 percent of families enroll their children in primary and secondary schools.

Muslims in Iran follow very strict rules about the clothes they wear, the food they eat, and the way they act in public. Men wear long, loose-fitting pants and shirts with collars (long sleeves are preferred). Beginning at the age of seven, women must cover themselves with a long, hooded robe called a *chador*, meaning "tent," when they are in public.

Muslims worship their god, *Allah*, in *mosques*. Most mosques have tall towers called *minarets*. From the top of the minaret, men call the people to the mosque to pray. Muslims pray five times every day: at dawn, noon, mid-afternoon, sunset, and 90 minutes after sunset.

Above: School boys in Esfahan returning home from a day at school.

Right: Minarets, like this one at the Great Mosque in Esfahan, were used to call Muslims throughout the city to their daily prayers

Stop 5: Bandar-e Abbas

Bandar-e Abbas sits on the southern coast of Iran overlooking the Strait of Hormuz, a thin strip of water that separates Iran from the southern Persian Gulf countries of Oman and the United Arab Emirates. Bandar-e Abbas is Iran's most important port city.

Bandar-e Abbas began as a small fishing village called Gamerun. Today, it is the only international port along the northern shores of the Persian Gulf. The size and population of the city have grown steadily as the shipping facilities have improved.

The people of Bandar-e Abbas and the surrounding coastal areas are called *Bandaris*. They descend from a mixture of Arab and African ancestors, and their traditions of dress and language differ from those of other Iranians. The women of Minab, just east of Bandar-e Abbas, wear a hard mask called a *borca*, which covers most of the face.

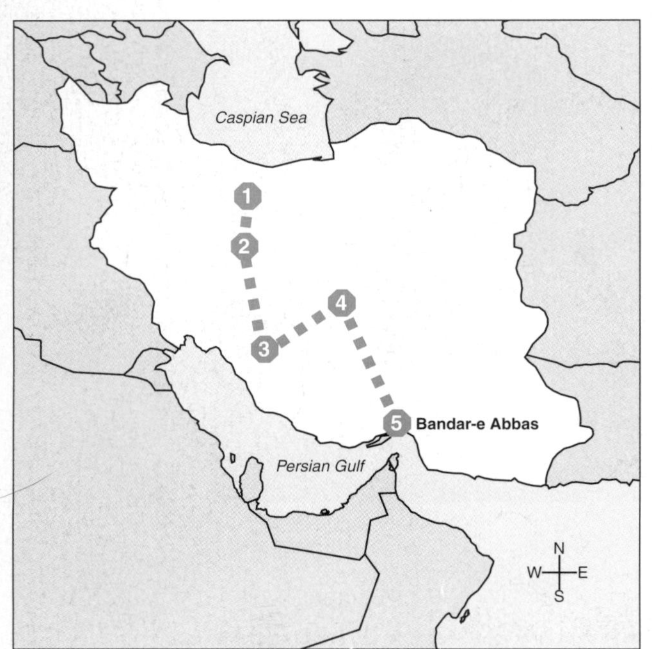

Now let's fly ***northeast*** *to Bam.*

Above: A view of the lagoon on Hormuz Island in the Persian Gulf.

Right: A man dries fish on the island of Hormuz in the Persian Gulf.

Stop 6: Bam

Date palms and eucalyptus trees line the main streets of the *oasis* town of Bam, located at the southern end of the Dasht-e-Lut desert. In the harsh deserts of central and southern Iran, small groves of trees grow in isolated places where water is available. Sometimes, these oases become small villages or towns.

Bam has two parts: the modern downtown area, and the original city and fortress, called Arg-e Bam. The fortress and original city were built between 224 and 637 C.E., enclosed within a wall. From the top of the wall, a person can look out over the old and new portions of the town.

Until the 1930's, the fortress was used as barracks for the military. Today, only a small bookshop and tea house are there. Archaeologists are working to preserve and restore the site.

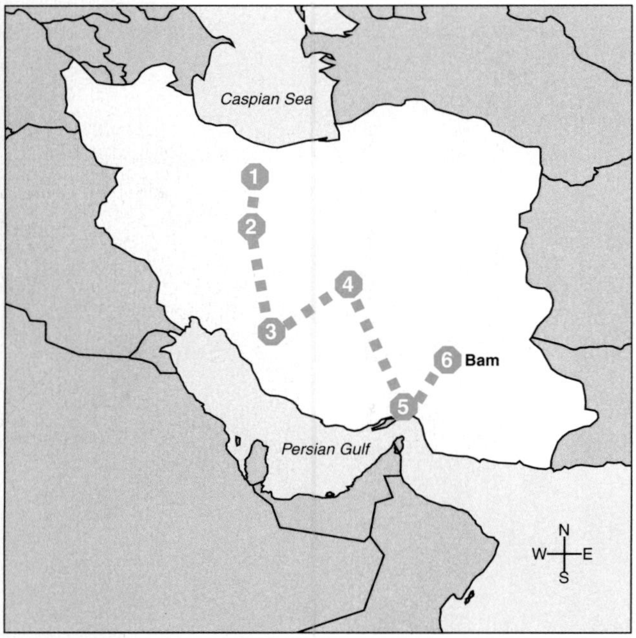

Now it is time to fly home.

Above: The fortress city of Bam, called Arg-e Bam.

Right: The ancient gate of the fortress city of Bam.

The Foods of Iran

Common ingredients in Iranian cooking are rice, bread, fresh vegetables, herbs, and fruits. Small portions of meat are often added for flavoring, but meat is not often served as a main course. Iranian cooking also uses dried fruits, nuts, and spices like cardamom and sumac to create a mixture of sweet and bitter tastes.

Breakfast might include a boiled or fried egg, a thin, oven-baked bread called *lavash* served with yoghurt, jam or honey, and tea. Yoghurt, called *mast*, is a common side dish, either mixed with other foods like rice or as a dip for bread.

During religious festivals and other occasions, families serve a traditional stew, or *khoresht*, called *fesenjan*. It consists of meat (duck, chicken, or lamb), vegetables, spices, and nuts served over rice. Other dishes include *kuku*, (a thick omelette served hot or cold), *kabab* (a thin strip of roasted meat), and *dolme* (stuffed vegetable, fruit, or vine leaves, filled with rice, vegetables, and meat).

Above: Fried eggs and lavash, a thin, dry bread, are common breakfast foods.

Right: A young boy helps out in a bakery. Families in Iran purchase fresh bread daily for their meals.

Glossary

Allah The God of Islam.

badgir A tower built to funnel wind through a house.

bazaar A large shopping mall.

borca A hard, inflexible mask worn by women in Minab.

chador A long, hooded robe worn by women.

ghanat An underground tunnel that channels water through the desert.

minaret A tall tower attached to a mosque used to call people to prayers.

mosque An Islamic church where Muslims worship Allah, their God.

oasis A small pocket of plantlife and water in the middle of a dry desert.

relief A type of sculpture that creates an image by carving away the surrounding surface of the stone.

scavenger An animal that eats other animals that have died.

Further Reading

Department of Geography, Lerner Publications, ed. *Iran in Pictures*. Minneapolis: Lerner Publications, 1989.

Fox, Mary Virginia. *Iran*. Chicago: Children's Press, 1991.

Greenway, Paul. *Iran*. Hawthorne, Victoria, Australia: Lonely Planet, 1998.

Lyle, Garry. *Iran*. Philadelphia: Chelsea House, 1997.

O'Shea, Maria. *Culture Shock!: Iran*. Portland: Graphic Arts Center Publishing Company, 1999.

Suggested Web Sites

Excite Travel: Destinations: Iran
<http://www.excite.com/travel/countries/iran/>

Iranian Cultural and Information Center
<http://www.tehran.stanford.edu>

Salam Iran HomePage
<http://www.salamiran.org>
<http://www.roadstoruins.com>

Index

Acknowledgments and Photo Credits
Cover: © Rex Fritschi; pp. 11, 15 (top), 16, 21, 27, 29 (below): © Rex Fritschi; pp. 13, 23, 29: © Trip Photographic Library/M. Good; pg. 13 (inset): © Trip Photographic Library/Christopher Rennie; pg. 15: © Trip Photographic Library/J. Sweeney; pg. 19: © A. Griffin/American Stock Photography; pg. 25: © Trip Photographic Library/M. Cerny.

Maps: Moritz Design.